this is NEW ZEALAND

this is NEW ZEALAND

REED

Published by Reed Books, a division of Reed Publishing (NZ) Ltd, 39 Rawene Rd, Birkenhead, Auckland. Associated companies, branches and representatives throughout the world.

ISBN 0 7900 0645 6

© 1998
First published in 1992 and 1997 as *This is New Zealand* and *Introducing New Zealand*

The authors assert their moral rights in the work.

Design by Sunny H. Yang
Cover photograph of Lake Matheson by Noel Bartley

Printed in Hong Kong

CONTENTS

Aotearoa — Land of Long White Cloud

The North Island

The South Island

AoteaRoa —
LAND OF THE LONG WHITE CLOUD

Venturing into the Southern Pacific Ocean around 1,200 years ago, the great Polynesian navigator Kupe found a new land. Legend holds that his first sight was not of the land itself, but of a long white cloud that hovered above it, and so he named it Aotearoa: Land of the Long White Cloud. Today the land is usually known as New Zealand, although Aotearoa is the recognised Maori name for the country.

The Land

New Zealand is a unique land, sitting in isolation on the edge of the Southwest Pacific. To the south is Antarctica, and the Pacific Ocean stretches east over 8,000 km to the South American coast. To the north lie the tiny and scattered Pacific Islands, and nearly 2,000 km to the west is Australia.

Comparatively, New Zealand is similar in size to Great Britain or the American state of Colorado. Two main islands, the North and the South, account for nearly all of the 269,000 sq km area of New Zealand. A much smaller and sparsely populated third, Stewart Island, lies just south of the South Island. New Zealand is a long thin land, covering around 1,500 km from the top of the North Island to the bottom of Stewart Island. At its widest point, across the middle of the North Island, it is 450 km. However, no inland point is more than 120 km from the sea. Over 15,000 km of coastline surround the land, varying from long, easily accessible sandy beaches to spectacular fiords.

In geological terms New Zealand is a young land. It lies along the faultline between the Pacific and Indian Plates and was pushed up from the sea floor around ten to fifteen million years ago. The action of the two plates has thrown up a predominantly mountainous land, with 223 peaks higher then 2,300 metres; approximately three-quarters of the land is more than 200 metres above sea level. Although the land lies along a faultline, geological and volcanic activity is only moderate.

The Southern Alps dominate the South Island, forming a picturesque region of mountain peaks, glaciers, lakes and fiords, centred around the 3,754-metre Mt Cook, known to Maori as Aoraki. The North Island was mainly formed by volcanic activity, and volcanoes, only a few of which are still active, are common. Mt Ruapehu, sitting almost in the centre of the island, is the largest. It erupted in 1996 and 1997, and continues to throw up rocks and spectacular ash clouds. New Zealand's most active volcano, White Island, lies off the Bay of Plenty coast.

In addition to volcanoes, the faultline running through the North Island also created a number of dramatic thermal regions. The most famous are in the town of Rotorua and near Lake Taupo.

Although mountains dominate, the unique nature of New Zealand means that nearly every kind of landform can be found. The Southern Alps give way in the east and south to rolling foothills and the large, fertile plains of Canterbury and Southland. On the other side of the mountains the West Coast is famed for its wild, rugged forests. Centuries of volcanic activity also gave the North Island large areas of fertile farmland, while extensive commercial forests cover other areas.

Climate

The fertile lands of New Zealand are complemented by a near perfect climate. The country is in the temperate zone, roughly the antipodes of Spain, Portugal and parts of France, but its isolated oceanic location provides a varied yet mild climate.

In general, summers are rarely too hot or winters too cold. The extreme length of the country means that there is some variety, but the oceanic weather patterns tend to prevent extreme conditions. In Northland, nicknamed 'the winterless north', average summer temperatures are around 25° Celsius, and in Southland the winter averages are around 1° Celsius. The mountainous regions of the Alps and the central North Island experience

colder temperatures, but snowfalls are rare beyond the mountains and never occur in most areas.

While the oceanic climate prevents extreme conditions, it also means the weather is very changeable and often windy. Most areas receive over 2,000 hours of sunshine a year, but it can also rain at any time, although mainly in winter.

Flora and Fauna

The uniqueness of the land is matched by unique plants and animals. New Zealand's separation from the rest of the world meant indigenous life also developed separately, free of most of the competition and predators that affected evolution elsewhere.

Evergreen native forests once covered the land and contained some of the most ancient plants on earth. Giant, slow-growing kauri, rimu and totara dominated the forests, along with an indigenous beech tree. Human habitation led to extensive forest clearance for agriculture, especially after the arrival of Europeans. Only around a quarter of the original indigenous forests (six million hectares) still remain, and recent conservation efforts should protect what is left. However, faster-growing introduced trees have taken over elsewhere and make regeneration of native forests difficult.

13

As with the trees, the native vegetation and flowering plants are unlike anywhere else in the world. In particular the rare flora of the sub-alpine regions attract botanists from all over the globe. The mixture of native cabbage trees, flax, toetoe, ferns and nikau palms that occur across New Zealand is unique, and the brilliant yellow flowers of the kowhai and the red of the rata and pohutukawa give a New Zealand spring its own particular style.

Aside from two species of small bat New Zealand has no indigenous mammals. Devoid of large land predators, flightless birds developed unmolested. The largest, the moa, is now extinct, but two nocturnal flightless birds still exist. The kakapo is a large parrot, and there are several species of the bird adopted as New Zealand's national emblem, the kiwi.

Along with the flightless varieties there are also hundreds of other birds, from seabirds such as penguins and albatrosses to the musical tui and bellbird. There are a number of parrots, the best known being the world's only mountain parrot, the kea. It has spectacular

colours, and an inquisitive and sometimes destructive nature.

Among New Zealand's many species of small reptiles the most notable is the tuatara. Fossils show tuatara were around during the age of the dinosaur. New Zealand does not have any snakes, indigenous or introduced.

Over 20,000 different species of insects, snails, spiders and worms are also indigenous to the land, and 90 percent are unique. The weta is one of the most ancient lifeforms in the world, believed to have been unchanged for 190 million years. At 71 grams the giant weta is also the largest insect in the world yet, despite a fearsome appearance, it is harmless. The katipo, a mildly poisonous spider found only in the north, is the only venomous animal in New Zealand.

The moderate climate and fertile land helped introduced species flourish. Forestry and domestic animals, such as cattle and sheep, became major contributors to the economy, but other introduced animals and plants are considered noxious. Predators such as cats, rats

New Zealand is home to the world's only mountain parrot, the kea. Fossil evidence has shown tuatara (right) were around during the age of the dinosaur.

and stoats attack native birds, while rabbits, possums, goats and deer devastate the vegetation and forests. Introduced plants such as gorse, broom and various weeds are also a problem.

Conservation and environmental controls have become important, particularly as New Zealanders have always taken pride in living in a 'clean, green' country. Extensive efforts are being made to protect the indigenous species that are still left. Offshore islands are being turned into sanctuaries and laws protecting native trees from wholesale logging have been enacted, while stringent border controls prevent the entry of more pests. Concern for the environment also led to the establishment of a Department of Conservation, and a number of anti-pollution measures such as the introduction of lead-free petrol, the banning of imported CFCs, and the encouragement to recycle.

History

As Maori did not have a written language, New Zealand's history prior to the arrival of Europeans is sketchy. What is known is derived from archaeological evidence and the rich mix of myth and legend that is Maori folklore.

Once settlements were established, Maori developed a strong social structure based around tribal and family associations. The majority of the population settled in the warmer north, combining horticulture with fishing and hunting birds in the forest. Tribal warfare was common and a proud warrior tradition developed.

Although their tools were of a stone-age technology, Maori still created magnificent ornaments from stone and greenstone (pounamu), and were accomplished woodcarvers and

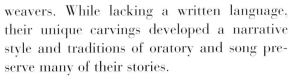

weavers. While lacking a written language, their unique carvings developed a narrative style and traditions of oratory and song preserve many of their stories.

In 1642 the Dutch navigator Abel Tasman sighted and mapped parts of the West Coast,

17

giving the land the name Nieuw Zeeland after a region of the Netherlands. However, it was not until 1769 that Europeans returned. The first voyage of the English navigator James Cook led to New Zealand's circumnavigation and mapping. This, and two subsequent visits by Cook, opened New Zealand to the rest of the world and established its links with Britain.

The first Europeans to settle were whalers and sealers, who chased the abundant herds of the southern oceans. They were followed by missionaries, and by the 1830s a number of settlements had been established. While there were some tensions and violent incidents between Maori and Europeans, in general the early contacts were friendly.

New Zealand's climate and fertile lands attracted more permanent settlers and, in England in particular, the pressure to colonise began. At the end of the 1830s the British Government, partly worried that other nations like France would get in first, decided to seek formal sovereignty over the country. In 1840 William Hobson arrived in the Bay of Islands to offer a treaty on behalf of the Crown. At the same time many Maori had realised that increasing European settlement was inevitable and the offer of British protection was accepted.

The Treaty of Waitangi

On 6 February 1840, at Waitangi, William Hobson and a large number of Maori chiefs signed what became known as the Treaty of Waitangi. The Treaty was taken through the country and eventually signed by over 500 chiefs. As New Zealand does not have a written constitution the Treaty is generally accepted as its founding document, and 6 February is a national holiday.

The Treaty has caused controversies that are still alive today. Differing interpretations by Maori and the Crown were not helped by the existence of two Treaties, one in English and one in Maori. An imprecise translation created subtle differences between the two and fuelled disputes over what Maori had agreed to give to the Crown and what they still retained sovereignty over. Some of these disputes continue today.

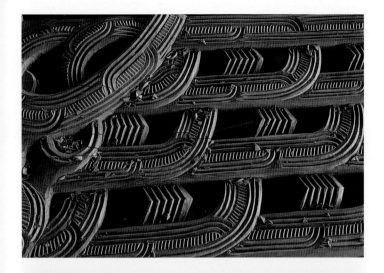

However, in 1840 the Treaty's immediate effect was to open up New Zealand for colonisation. Initially, most colonists settled in the South Island, which had a smaller Maori population and excellent land for wool production. The discovery of gold in Otago and on the West Coast increased the attraction of the South Island, and until the turn of the century it held the majority of the population. Since then the North Island has taken over, today only a quarter of the population live in the South.

Increasing colonisation led to demands for more land and the pressure on Maori to sell increased. A number of unscrupulous and unfair land deals were made and some Maori tried to limit the sales. Inevitably European demand for land, and Maori reluctance to sell, led to violence. Through the 1860s and early 1870s there were a series of conflicts that have become known as the Land Wars.

Most of the fighting was in the central North Island. Although the Land Wars could not be called a full civil war, there were a number of pitched battles and campaigns. Not all Maori fought against the Government, some tribes opted to support them.

British technology and weight of numbers were eventually too much for their opponents, but not before Maori had given a good account of themselves. They often surprised the British with clever tactics and were capable of confounding superior numbers. While in the end the Government won, certain areas were never actually conquered and a number of Maori leaders were never caught. There was in fact no victory or exact moment at which the wars could be said to have ended; Maori resistance gradually tapered off in the late 1860s and early 1870s.

A Growing Independence

By the end of the 1870s the country was peaceful and the population had increased to half a million. Railways and roads were under construction and in 1882 the first shipment of frozen meat left Port Chalmers aboard the *Dunedin*. Its arrival in England heralded the beginning of New Zealand's large meat and dairy exporting industries.

As settlers cut into the forests, establishing the farms that are still central to the economy, the New Zealand of the nineteenth century could be described as a pioneer nation. By the end of the century the country was also developing a reputation as a social pioneer. Regulation and protection of working conditions, injury compensation, compulsory

Since the 1970s Kiri Te Kanawa has been one of the world's leading sopranos.

New Zealander Jean Batten broke several aviation records during the 1920s and 1930s.

arbitration of industrial disputes and state loans to people buying farms were introduced. In 1893 New Zealand became the first nation in the world to give the vote to women and in 1898 old age pensions were instituted.

In 1907 the colony was granted Dominion status and the twentieth century saw the New Zealand economy and standard of living grow. Most New Zealanders, including many Maori, were fiercely loyal to the British Empire, England being referred to as the home country. Consequently New Zealand did not hesitate to follow Britain into World War I. Thousands of men went to war and by 1918 New Zealand had suffered more casualties per head of population than any other country.

The war also started the gradual process whereby New Zealand left Britain's protection becoming a truly independent nation. Although a few New Zealanders had fought in the Boer War, World War I was the first time the country had sent its army to fight, and pride in the endeavours of New Zealand troops fuelled a national patriotism separate from Imperial sentiments. April 25, the day in 1915 when New Zealand troops first went into action, has become a national day of remembrance.

As the twentieth century saw New Zealand step out in the world as a nation, so it also saw individual New Zealanders make their mark. Early in the century Ernest Rutherford split the atom, and in 1908 he won the Nobel Prize, while in the 1920s and 1930s Jean Batten was breaking international aviation records.

Like the rest of the world, New Zealand was hit hard by the Depression. In 1935 it elected a Labour Government which promised more pioneering social reform, social security and the 40-hour working week, a comprehensive health system and State-funded housing programmes were introduced.

World War II again saw New Zealand commit large numbers of men, nearly ten percent of the population going to fight overseas. Like their World War I counterparts, these troops gained fearsome reputations in Crete, North Africa, Italy and the Pacific.

The post-war period was a boom time for the New Zealand economy. With Europe devastated by the war the agricultural wealth of New Zealand was in demand. The 1950s saw full employment, and industry started to develop.

More New Zealanders rose to international prominence as well. Edmund Hillary conquered Mt Everest in 1953. The 1960s and 1970s saw middle-distance runners Peter Snell and John Walker continue a tradition of Olympic victory and world records that had been started by Jack Lovelock in 1936. Photographer Brian Brake established himself internationally, and since the 1970s Kiri Te Kanawa has been one of the world's leading sopranos. The tradition continues today; in 1994 film director Jane Campion and twelve-year-old Anna Paquin became the first New Zealanders to win Academy Awards with the movie *The Piano*, and at the 1996 Olympics swimmer Danyon Loader and equestrian Blyth Tait won gold for their country.

Social reforms have also continued. The Accident Compensation Act of 1972 guaranteed insurance to anyone injured by accident, and the Homosexual Law Reform Act, removing discrimination, was passed in 1986. Ombudsmen, a Race Relations Conciliator, an Equal Opportunities Tribunal and a Privacy Commissioner have been established to protect individual rights, while Maori grievances over land disputes and the Treaty of Waitangi led to the establishment of the Waitangi Tribunal to investigate claims.

Economically, however, New Zealand deteriorated through the 1970s and 1980s. Because of its size and lack of mineral resources, New Zealand has always relied heavily on imports, especially of fuel. Consequently the oil shocks of the 1970s hit New Zealand hard. Also,

despite some industrial development, New Zealand was still reliant on primary production such as meat, dairy and wool exports, with the United Kingdom as its major market. After Britain entered the European Community in the early 1970s, New Zealand started to lose its traditional export markets.

Lacking strong industries and with a heavily subsidised agricultural sector, New Zealand became uncompetitive internationally. The 1980s saw another Labour Government institute wide-ranging reforms. Monetary policies were introduced, industry was deregulated, subsidies cut and many government departments privatised. Gradually the economy began to recover.

New Zealand in the Pacific

New Zealand's traditionally strong role in the Pacific began in 1901 when Britain passed the administration of the Cook Islands and Niue to this country. The outbreak of World War I saw New Zealand troops occupy German possessions in the Pacific and take control of Western Samoa. New Zealand continued to govern these islands until they gained independence, and Niueans and Cook Islanders still retain New Zealand citizenship. The Tokelaus are the only dependency still under New Zealand administration, but links with the other Pacific Islands are still strong.

New Zealand is a leading member of regional organisations and continues to provide support in the Pacific; half of all New Zealand's overseas aid is spent assisting Pacific nations. Similarly, the Islands tend to see New Zealand as their strongest ally. Many Pacific Islanders have moved to New Zealand, and today Auckland is the world's largest Polynesian city.

Like the Pacific Islands, New Zealand's connections with Australia have always been strong. For the first decade after the signing of the Treaty of Waitangi New Zealand was in fact governed from New South Wales.

Sporting contacts between the two nations have always been important, and recent years have also seen moves to improve economic ties under the Closer Economic Relations (CER) agreement. Travel between the two countries is regular and many New Zealanders live and work in Australia, as do many Australians in New Zealand.

Despite its size New Zealand has been prominent internationally. In 1984 it declared itself nuclear-free, and it has been a leading proponent of disarmament ever since. The country is active in the United Nations and its organisations. It has been a frequent member of the Security Council and over fifteen percent of the armed forces have served as peacekeepers in places such as Bosnia, the Middle East, Cambodia, and Angola. It also plays a part in most major international economic organisations, and in the conservation and administration of the Antarctic.

Society

A s the land of Aotearoa is geologically young, so also is the nation of New Zealand. Politically it is still developing its own independent institutions, and over half of the 3.6 million population is under 35.

When the Treaty of Waitangi was signed in 1840 one of its provisions was to recognise the British Sovereign, Queen Victoria, as New Zealand's ruler. English colonisation then established institutions modelled on British ideas of democracy. The British influence has remained strong and Queen Elizabeth II is still officially New Zealand's Head of State. Similarly, immigrants continue to make up a significant proportion of New Zealanders.

Queen Elizabeth II is officially recognised as New Zealand's Head of State.

The Political System

Prior to European arrival, Maori lived in separate tribal groups. While there was regular interaction between tribes, Maori identified solely with their individual tribe and there was no national leader or political organisation. After 1840, British government was embraced by many Maori. Unlike many other colonial nations, and assisted by the spirit of the Treaty of Waitangi, the political rights of Maori were recognised. In 1867 four seats in parliament were set aside for Maori only. Since then Maori have had the option of voting either in their local general electorate or in a regional Maori electorate.

The Honorable Jenny Shipley, New Zealand's first woman Prime Minister, was sworn in on 8 December 1997.

Although Maori seats in parliament and Maori Land Courts were established, the majority of such institutions remained direct reflections of their British counterparts. This adherence to British traditions has remained well into the twentieth century, and even today there are still a lot of similarities with the United Kingdom.

Technically New Zealand is a Constitutional Monarchy with the Queen of England as the official Head of State. A Governor-General, usually a prominent and respected New Zealander, is appointed by the Queen to act as her representative. In practice, however, neither the Crown nor the Governor-General has any real power. The effective head of state is the Prime Minister, and the Governor-General's role is largely ceremonial.

There is only one chamber in parliament and elections are held every three years. The party, or coalition of parties, which holds the majority in parliament forms the government, the leader of that party becoming Prime Minister and its senior members forming the cabinet. The Prime Minister and cabinet must all be elected members of parliament.

The judicial system of jury trials and the presumption of innocence is also very similar to the United Kingdom. So much so that until recently the British Privy Council was still recognised as New Zealand's highest court. Like Britain, New Zealand also remains one of the few nations whose police force does not carry guns.

New Zealand's parliamentary building is located in the capital city of Wellington and is known as the 'Beehive'.

The Kiwi Personality

While major institutions have British origins, New Zealand has always had its own personality. Typically for a pioneering nation, the early colonists were largely classless. Primarily, many came to New Zealand to escape an English society dominated by class and landed gentry. Because of this, New Zealand developed a proudly egalitarian population. This attitude is still very strong and is often described as part of the national psyche. One result of this egalitarianism is that New Zealanders have gained a reputation as informal, friendly people.

Another legacy of New Zealand's pioneering days is a pride in self-reliance and pragmatism. The isolation of the pioneers meant that when problems occurred the usual remedies were not always immediately available. Ingenious solutions had to be found with whatever materials were at hand, and this developed into a tradition often dubbed 'Kiwi ingenuity'. New Zealanders are still proud of their reputation for innovation, and the agricultural sector in particular has benefited greatly from home-grown inventions.

Free of the vested interests of the old world and dominated by egalitarian sentiments, New Zealand also embraced social reforms. From the 1930s to the late 1980s wide-ranging social security protection was a major part of New Zealand's welfare system. The economic problems of the 1980s, however, and the introduction of monetarist policies, led to changes. While New Zealand's social security provisions still rank high in international comparisons, they are no longer as extensive as they were. Public hospitals still provide free care for major medical problems and primary and secondary education is free and guaranteed to all, with children required to stay at school until they are sixteen. However, university and polytechnic students are now required to pay fees.

Although more egalitarian than Britain, New Zealand's strong links to England remained for many years. For a long time England was literally called 'home' by New Zealanders. References to Britain as 'the home country' continued even into the 1960s as immigrants were almost exclusively British, although at times there were brief influxes of Danish, Dalmatian, Dutch and other European immigrants. These nationalities brought their own cultural traditions and even retained some of these in their local communities, but on the whole they were quickly assimilated into the English-dominated society.

During both World Wars Australia and New Zealand co-operated closely. The wars had similar effects on the two countries' movement towards true independence. Along with the social and political upheavals that occurred globally, the wars had unique effects in the South Pacific.

ANZAC troops sent to fight in Europe during World War I reflected the egalitarian values of New Zealand and Australia, while the British army they fought alongside was still dominated by class. In addition, coming from predominantly rural backgrounds, the New Zealand and Australian troops were often physically stronger and healthier then their allies. The ANZACs quickly gained proud reputations in battle and many of them had a low regard for the abilities of the other soldiers. This was combined with a belief that the upper class British High Command regarded colonials as inferior and used them as cannon fodder in campaigns such as Gallipoli. Many of the troops returned from the war resenting their treatment by the British.

After the war New Zealand gradually became a more independent nation. Ties with Britain did remain strong through the next few decades; when World War II broke out New Zealand was again one of the first countries to join the Allies. The Japanese attack on Pearl Harbour and the advance through South East Asia and the Pacific was traumatic for New Zealand and Australia. Both countries had taken it for granted that if they were under threat Britain would come to their aid. Britain, however, was concentrating on the war in Europe and the ineffective forces they had in the Pacific were easily swept aside. It was American troops who came to the rescue. While the effect of Britain's failure to defend New Zealand was not immediately obvious, after the war New Zealand's international focus started shifting away from Britain and Europe to the Pacific, Asia and America.

During the 1960s just over 50 percent of New Zealand's exports went to Britain; today as little as 6 percent go to Britain.

As New Zealanders have started to see themselves as an Asian-Pacific nation, they have also slowly started to change their institutions. In 1987 Maori was made an official language alongside English. It is now taught in most schools and there are also Maori language only schools.

The 1990s have seen this gradual process of change accelerate, the biggest break with English tradition occurring in 1996. New Zealand's parliament had been based on the Westminster system of electing representatives to local electorates, or 'seats', the party with the most seats becoming the government. However, from 1996 New Zealand's system of government changed to Mixed Member Proportional (MMP) representation.

Under the new system half the seats in parliament are still chosen as electorates. The rest are allocated to the parties based on the

proportion of votes cast for each party. The new system has also seen the number of seats overall rise from 96 to 120.

The impetus for change did not stop with MMP. Prior to 1996 New Zealand awards for service to the community were also borrowed from Britain. They have now been replaced by the Order of New Zealand. There is also a small but growing republican movement wanting to cut all links with the British Crown and replace the Governor-General with a President.

As New Zealand has changed its focus away from the traditional links to Britain, so the origins of immigrants have changed. Since the 1960s the numbers arriving from Britain have dropped to negligible levels. The 1970s saw massive Polynesian immigration, in part promoted by the government and in part due to the prospects of better jobs and pay than were

available in the Islands. This immigration was such that there are now more Niueans and Cook Islanders in New Zealand than in their home countries.

The late 1980s and early 1990s saw a sizeable number of immigrants from Asia, particularly of Chinese descent. However, the overall rate of immigration has fallen significantly since the 1970s.

While recent years have seen a change in immigration, nearly 75 percent of the population are of European or Pakeha (the Maori word for European New Zealanders) descent and just under 13 percent are Maori. Polynesians make up 3.5 percent of the population, with 2 percent Asian and Chinese.

Since World War II the population has become more urbanised. Over one million people live in Auckland; the capital, Wellington, and Christchurch each have a population of over 300,000. Hamilton and Dunedin are the other cities with populations greater than 100,000.

Tangata Whenua — the People of the Land

Maori have always had a deep attachment to the land and their traditions. Even though western influences are strong, the strength of this attachment has meant that Maoritanga (Maori culture) retains a prominent role in New Zealand. Many Maori continue to keep their language, culture and traditions alive, and in turn those traditions play a large part in creating the unique nature of New Zealand.

Like all races, Maori have their own mythology and religion. Traditional beliefs were that all living things 'people, plants and animals', were descended from the gods. The gods were

trapped by the embrace of their father, Ranginui, and mother, Papa-tua-nuku. After they were separated by Tane, one of the gods, Ranginui became the sky and Papa-tua-nuku the earth. Tane then created the trees, bushes and creatures, and finally, from the earth, he created the first woman, Hine-ahu-one. The daughter of Hine-ahu-one and Tane, Hine-titama, unaware that Tane was her father, also bore him children who became the first ancestors of all humans.

After the gods came the great hero Maui. A rogue and a trickster, Maui also had magical powers. There are many myths surrounding Maui's adventures, three of the most popular telling how he discovered fire, slowed the sun to make the days longer, and fished the North Island out of the sea.

After the great navigator Kupe discovered Aotearoa, the first Maori settlers arrived aboard a number of great ocean-going canoes, or waka. They came from an island called Hawaiki, believed to have been somewhere in what is now French Polynesia. The settlers became the nuclei of the first iwi (tribes), and most Maori are still able to trace their ancestry back through their iwi to one of the waka. As Maori spread through Aotearoa each iwi came to feel great reverence for the land on which they lived. As Maori people are the tangata whenua of New Zealand, so also is each iwi the tangata whenua of its traditional lands.

The concept of a Maori nationality did not exist before the arrival of Europeans, and in fact it was European usage of the word Maori that led to it becoming the name of the Polynesian inhabitants of New Zealand. Maori referred to themselves in terms of their tribal affiliations, and many still continue this tradition today.

The Marae

Maori society revolves around the marae, the focus of which is the whare whakairo (the meeting house) and the open area directly in front of it. The whare whakairo represents the unity of its local community and its design is symbolic of the human form. It is always named after a respected ancestor, while the decoration and carving of the building hold special meanings or tell stories relevant to the marae. The open ground in front symbolises the land from which an iwi derives its identity and mana (or prestige). Because of the spiritual significance of the marae, strict protocols govern behaviour on it.

Originally Maori lived on, or close to, the marae and this continued for most Maori into

the twentieth century. Although this has changed in recent years, the importance of the marae in Maori society remains. Major social, political and ceremonial functions still take place on marae, and it often has a role in assisting welfare groups working with Maori.

The Treaty of Waitangi is very important to Maori and its signing in 1840 is significant for many reasons. The Treaty ceded the country to the British crown, was the catalyst for colonisation and the moment modern New Zealand began. But the Treaty also guaranteed Maori people citizenship and protected their rights, privileges and possessions.

While Maori embraced many western methods and ideas, in particular Christianity, colonisation also had harmful effects. After the

signing of the Treaty Maori retained their independence and self government, but as Pakeha pressure for more land increased and led to war, so also did the curbs on Maori independence increase. After the Land Wars British law took precedence and the removal of land from Maori ownership increased. The significance of land to Maori meant its loss was also a loss of mana, which in turn increased feelings of disenfranchisement. Additionally, as Maori

society was mainly agrarian, losing the land led to economic and social problems. Around the turn of the century a number of highly educated Maori politicians and leaders did improve matters in rural areas, but Maori had lost any effective influence on the rest of New Zealand life.

Maori also experienced a number of problems typical of colonialism. Western diseases and warfare affected the population so much that by the end of the nineteenth century it was believed Maori would eventually die out. Meanwhile, patronising racial attitudes and beliefs in European superiority led to a policy of assimilation. Maori were encouraged, occasionally even forced, to speak English, forget their customs and adopt western lifestyles. These attitudes lasted well into the twentieth century.

A Maori Renaissance

Until World War II many Maori remained within their traditional rural communities, but the post-war period saw a large urban migration. This caused much dislocation and many Maori lost touch with their heritage, consequently social problems increased. However, this increased national awareness of Maori and helped galvanise action groups wanting to change public attitudes. In the 1970s a Maori Renaissance, led mainly by young educated urban Maori, gained momentum. Maori culture, arts and language have since undergone revivals which continue today.

Along with the cultural revival there was also a political revival. Wounds over land lost since 1840 had never healed and calls to redress Maori grievances increased. This issue was brought to prominence in 1975 with a hikoi, or land march, from Northland to Parliament in Wellington, which was followed by a number of

high profile land occupations. The Waitangi Tribunal was established in 1975 to investigate contemporary disputes over breaches of the Treaty of Waitangi and in 1985 it was expanded to consider grievances dating back to 1840. A process of compensation was initiated and the return of some land has begun.

From the first Maori settlement tribal warfare was common, and it continued after first contacts with Europeans. Maori were proud of their abilities as warriors, and even Captain Cook noted the strong physical condition of the people. Though colonisation eventually saw an end to intertribal wars, the warrior spirit of the Maori remained. During the Land Wars Maori devised ingenious tactics to combat their opponents' superior firepower. They impressed the Europeans with their soldiering ability, and leaders such as Rewi Maniapoto won respect for their generalship.

The warrior spirit was revived during the World Wars. In World War II a Maori Battalion was formed and fought in North Africa and Europe, gaining a fearsome reputation along the way.

The warrior spirit is also credited as being one of the reasons Maori took to the sportsfields, especially the rugby field, so readily after European settlement. Since the late nineteenth century Maori have been prominent in almost every sport played in New Zealand, and many of New Zealand's greatest sportspeople have been Maori.

Games, gardens
and Godzone

N ew Zealanders enjoy an enviable lifestyle. The small population and abundance of land has allowed cities to spread out, and nearly every home has room for a garden. New Zealanders are also passionate sportspeople, renowned internationally as fierce competitors in nearly every major sport, especially the national game of rugby. The combination of the easy lifestyle, the mild climate and the beauty of the land led early New Zealanders to describe the land as 'God's Own Country'; today it is still sometimes referred to as 'Godzone'.

Sport

There is nothing that galvanises national pride more than a New Zealand competitor or team beating the rest of the world in a sporting contest. Larger countries like the United States or Japan dominate international affairs and it is difficult for a small country like New Zealand to have an impact. However, in sport New Zealand competes on equal terms with the bigger nations.

The importance of sport goes beyond national pride. Early New Zealand lacked the sophistication of Europe and, especially in rural areas, sporting competitions were often the only entertainment available. Often the social

benefits of sport were greater then the games themselves and the sports field has become a symbol of national unity as well as pride.

Sports fields can be found all over the country and every weekend nearly half the population will be out playing on them. New Zealanders will also try any sport, often regardless of barriers in their way: despite not having a single bobsled course in the entire country, New Zealanders have competed in the bobsled event at the Winter Olympics.

The National Game

From the Olympics to bungy jumping, America's Cup yachting to lawn bowls, New Zealanders have led the world. But no sport has meant more to the nation than rugby union. Drive into any town or city in the country and one of the first things you are likely to see is a pair of goalposts. Rugby holds a special place in New Zealand life. The physical nature of the sport suited the hard-working pioneers and although the first game was only played in 1870, by the 1890s it was being described as

the country's national game. Until the late 1960s it was virtually the only winter sport played by New Zealand men.

New Zealanders pride themselves on being the best rugby players in the world and are renowned for their hard, rugged style of play. The national team, the All Blacks, have dominated international rugby throughout the twentieth century and to be selected to play for them is still one of the greatest honours a New Zealander can achieve. They were also the first to wear the black uniforms and silver fern emblem that have since become national icons. There are about 580 rugby clubs in New Zealand, and over 150,000 people play the game at all levels and ages, from schoolchildren to senior citizens. Rugby league is also played, and while not as popular as rugby union, league does have a professional team, the Auckland Warriors, which competes in the Australian rugby league competition. Recent years have also seen a growth in women's rugby and touch rugby, which is played during summer when grounds are too hard for the full version.

Rugby is not the only sport at which New Zealanders excel. Except for the boycotted 1980 Moscow Games, New Zealanders have won at least one gold medal at every Olympics since 1952. Middle-distance runners have provided some of New Zealand's greatest moments. Jack Lovelock (1936), Peter Snell (1964) and John Walker (1976), all won gold in the 1500 metres. Snell also won the 800 metres in 1960 and 1964, while Murray

Halberg won the 5000 metres in 1960. Canoeing, rowing, yachting, swimming, equestrian, boxing and even field hockey teams have all returned victorious from the Olympics.

Because of their links with the sea New Zealanders are as skilled on water as on land. Auckland city is believed to have the highest proportion of boats per head of population of any city in the world. Canoeists have won five Olympic golds and rowers have won three. But the leading watersport is yachting.

One of the most popular pastimes in the country, New Zealand 'yachties' dominate the sport internationally, from small Olympic classes to the largest offshore boats. Along with numerous Olympic victories and world championships, New Zealanders have won the One Ton Cup, the Admiral's Cup and the last two Whitbread Round-the-World races. In 1995

New Zealand claimed the supreme yachting prize when a boat named *Black Magic*, and a team led by Whitbread victor Sir Peter Blake, challenged for and won the America's Cup.

New Zealanders have also performed well in equestrian three-day eventing. Mark Todd and his horse Charisma became sentimental favourites after they won both the 1984 and 1988 Olympic three-day events, and Blyth Tait won gold in the three-day event at the 1996 Olympics. Horse racing is another popular pastime and New Zealand's thoroughbred breeding industry is world famous.

It is not only men who have provided New Zealand with great sporting moments. Squash player Susan Devoy dominated her sport throughout the 1980s, winning the world championship on numerous occasions and the British Open for eight years in a row. The main women's team sport, netball, has around 100,000 participants, and the world champions title has been shared between New Zealand and Australia for the last two decades. At the Olympics Yvette Williams, who won the long jump in 1952, is the only New Zealander to win a field event, while Barbara Kendall's 1992 boardsailing victory completed a unique double with her brother Bruce, who won the

men's boardsailing in 1988. In 1997 Beatrice Faumuina won gold at the World Track and Field Champs held in Athens for discus, and in 1998 the New Zealand Women's Rugby Team won the Women's World Cup.

Women have also given New Zealand its own indigenous sport, marching. A team sport involving precision marching, it was invented during World War II as a way for young women to keep fit.

New Zealanders do not restrict themselves to team sports. The country boasts more golf courses per head of population than any other in the world, and in the 1960s British Open winner Bob Charles was one of the leading international players. Athletics, motor racing

and tennis are also popular, and successful competitors have included 1967 Formula One champion Denny Hulme, and the pre-World War I Wimbledon champion Anthony Wilding.

A more sedate sport, particularly popular with older people, is lawn bowls; the national championships is the biggest annual sports event in the country.

New Zealanders are not just satisfied with the major organised sports or refined pastimes. Ever since Sir Edmund Hillary and Sherpa Norgay Tenzing conquered Mt Everest, Kiwis have been leaders in adventure and endurance sports.

New Zealand's forests and mountains are much admired by trampers and climbers, while the fast-running, shallow rivers are perfect for canoeists, whitewater rafters and jet-boaters. The love of adventure reached a peak in the 1980s when bungy jumping was invented by New Zealander A.J. Hackett.

Triathlons, mountain biking and 'multi-sport' events are also very popular, including the South Island's annual 'Coast to Coast', a one-day race in which competitors run, canoe and cycle across the Southern Alps from the West Coast to Christchurch.

Tourism

The same mild climate and varied geography enjoyed by New Zealanders also attracts visitors from all over the world. The country provides tourists with a wide choice of activities, from the sedate to the adventurous, while New Zealanders' reputation for friendliness towards visitors is unparalleled.

The unique scenic beauty of the land can be enjoyed all year round and the country's thirteen national parks are geared toward people as well as conservation.

Some of the most dramatic natural features can be found in the North Island's thermal regions. The city of Rotorua is famous for its geysers and mudpools, while slightly further south near Taupo, another thermal region is complemented by the spectacular Huka Falls.

The Rotorua area is also the site of many old Maori settlements and, along with its thermal beauty, the city is renowned for its celebration of Maori tradition and culture. Performance groups and historic sites are integral parts of the region's attractions.

Tongariro National Park, in the central North Island, was the second national park to be established anywhere in the world (the first was Yellowstone Park in the United States). Its volcanoes dominate the area, providing not only scenic beauty, but skifields which usually operate well into spring.

In the north the Bay of Islands is popular with boating enthusiasts, as well as being home to the historic site where the Treaty of Waitangi was signed.

The West Coast of the South Island has a rugged and exciting coastline, while the Southern Alps are well known for their spectacular beauty. The lakeside resort of Queenstown is popular all year round and is a particular favourite with skiers, especially during its annual winter festival. Fiordland and Milford Sound are also renowned for their dramatic and beautiful scenery, and a variety of boat trips and scenic flights can be taken to explore the area. Scenic flights are also a feature in the Mount Cook region, including some which land on the Tasman Glacier.

Whale watching is one of the unique features of the east coast of the South Island. Whales migrating to the Antarctic pass by Kaikoura and special boat trips get incredibly close to the huge animals.

More active visitors enjoy getting even closer to the country's outdoors. New Zealand's forests, mountains and bush are loved by trampers and outdoor enthusiasts, with the Department of Conservation maintaining more than 10,000 km of walking tracks. The Abel Tasman coast track in the South Island is the most popular, with over 24,000 visitors annually, while the Milford and Routeburn Tracks are each walked by more than 10,000 people every year. Commercial guides can take visitors on easy, scenic hikes or provide more adventurous travellers with the challenges of wilder regions.

New Zealand's game fishing is world famous. The rivers of both islands are renowned for their trout, while the Bay of Islands is one of the finest deep sea fishing regions in the world.

Adventure tourism is another New Zealand speciality; whitewater rafting, jetboating, scuba diving, mountain climbing, extreme skiing and bungy jumping are all catered for and are popular with thrillseekers of all ages.

The country's twelve commercial skifields usually operate from May to October, and have occasionally been open into December. In addition most of the skifields are within easy reach of the ocean — at the right time of the year it is possible to go skiing in the morning and surfing in the afternoon.

Visitors to New Zealand can also experience the agricultural heritage of the land. The Agrodome, near Rotorua, and Mystery Creek just outside Hamilton, celebrate the dairy and sheep industries which the country's economy was built upon. For those who really want to get their hands dirty, 'farm-stay' holidays are available.

A feature of the New Zealand tourism industry is the way it caters for all budgets. Accommodation ranging from world class hotels to motels, camping grounds and a network of excellent backpacker hostels is available.

Getting About

New Zealanders' well-known friendliness also means backpackers rarely experience difficulties. However, the long thin nature of the land and the two islands do provide some challenges for travellers.

Because of the mountainous nature of New Zealand it was not until 1908 that the North Island was connected by the Main Trunk line from Auckland to Wellington, and a rail connection the length of the South Island took even longer. Today there are special scenic rail trips in the South Island, but many towns are not connected by rail. The limitations of rail travel are overcome by a number of commer-

cial bus networks, while travellers in a hurry can use the country's extensive airways.

One of the reasons New Zealand has a lot of air travel is Cook Strait, which separates the North and South Islands. The rough waters of the strait are the biggest barrier to any long distance travel through the country. However, the ferries which travel between Wellington and Picton are a feature of New Zealand life. The journey, which lasts a few hours, takes in the scenery of the Marlborough Sounds. Consequently the ferries are always popular, carrying over a million passengers annually.

Culture and Lifestyle

Maoritanga has a special place in New Zealand. The traditional skills of carving, weaving and performance arts remain strong and are supported financially by both government and private funding. New Zealanders also take pride in Maori traditions and many have been adopted by the nation. The best example is the haka, a traditional Maori challenge that was often performed before battle. Today many New Zealand sports teams, both national and local, perform a haka before their games.

While traditional performance groups continue to be popular, Maori performers do not restrict themselves to their traditional styles. Many of New Zealand's most popular modern entertainers, such as Sir Howard Morrison and the late Billy T. James, are Maori.

New Zealand's dramatic landscape and varied society have provided great inspiration for artists and writers. Painters such as C.F. Goldie, Frances Hodgkins, Colin McCahon, Ralph Hotere and Toss Woollaston have all drawn on the nation's unique qualities in their

For a country of such small size New Zealand has produced some outstanding writers including Witi Ihimaera (below), Booker Prize winner Keri Hulme, and Barry Crump (left).

work. The country's resources also provide materials for all manner of craft work. New Zealand potters, weavers, woodworkers and jewellers have developed international reputations, both for the quality of their work and for their use of indigenous materials.

Katherine Mansfield was the first New Zealand writer to gain international success in the early part of the twentieth century, but a distinct New Zealand style did not develop until much later. Since the 1960s writers such as Janet Frame, Maurice Gee, Maurice Shadbolt, Witi Ihimaera, Patricia Grace and Booker Prize winner Keri Hulme have all gained international reputations. Others such as Margaret Mahy and Joy Cowley are world leaders in children's writing. The pragmatic

New Zealand lifestyle is also celebrated in the books of Barry Crump, the cartoons of Murray Ball and the poems of Sam Hunt.

Reading is listed as a favourite pastime by nearly half of all New Zealanders. There are over 250 public libraries, with the National, Alexander Turnbull and Hocken libraries specialising in historical archives. The country also boasts 400 museums and art galleries.

The nation supports two full orchestras, a national ballet company and a number of professional theatres. There are also amateur theatrical societies, with a total of over 10,000 members. The electronic media is similarly well established. Three free national television channels are complemented by a number of local stations, pay TV channels and radio networks.

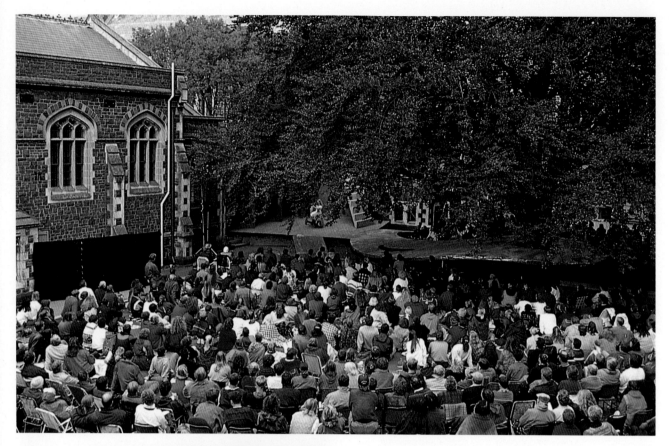

The climate encourages outdoor activities all year round and New Zealanders make the most of this. Gardening is one of the most popular leisure activities, and nearly every home has its own garden. Long summers mean that going to the beach, watersports, tramping and camping are also favourite pastimes. Barbecues and holidays at the beach are traditional and many families own a small summer home near a beach.

The geography complements the climate. No matter where you live you are always within two hours' drive of the sea, and forests, rivers and lakes are also all within easy reach. Although not as accessible, the country's mountains accommodate a number of excellent skifields.

The small population and relative abundance of land complete the natural benefits of the country. By international standards the cost of land is low, and the country's resources provide ample building materials. As a result a large percentage of homes are owned by their occupants, either through a mortgage or freehold. The mild climate keeps maintenance and heating costs down and, because of the nation's agricultural heritage, food prices are equally low.

Opened in February 1998, The Museum of New Zealand Te Papa Tongarewa was, during construction, the biggest such enterprise in the world. At a cost of $317 million the museum provides insight into New Zealand and her people; past, present and future.

Surrounded by Sheep

Farming has always dominated the New Zealand economy, to the extent that in the early 1980s there were 70 million sheep and only 3 million people in New Zealand. Although sheep numbers have dropped to under 50 million there are still 14 sheep for every person in New Zealand.

The Economy

The New Zealand economy is recovering after a downturn in the late 1970s and early 1980s. The mid-1980s saw major changes in economic policy. Government intervention was cut, industry deregulated, subsidies removed, government departments privatised and monetary policies were introduced to restrain inflation.

The economy was in flux for most of the 1980s. The new policies saw inflation and deficit levels fall, but unemployment rose dramatically and industrial production fell. The recovery began in 1991; unemployment has fallen steadily since then, and there has been strong economic growth. Strict monetary policies continue.

External trade dominates the economy. The country is not rich in minerals and so a lot of consumer products have to be imported. Manufactured goods form the bulk of imports.

Machinery, appliances and motor cars dominate, with fuels, medical, chemical and plastic imports also important. In contrast exports are dominated by primary products, around 60 percent of all exports coming from agriculture, fisheries and forestry. In 1994 meat exports alone accounted for one in every seven dollars of export earnings.

Traditionally Great Britain was New Zealand's major trading partner. In the 1960s, 50 percent of export and 40 percent of import trade was with the United Kingdom. Today, most trade is with Asian-Pacific nations. Australia, Japan and the United States are our three main trading partners. Other Asian countries take around 22 percent of exports, while only 16 percent go to the whole of Europe.

Farming

Even with the majority of the population living in cities, agriculture remains the mainstay of the economy. There are 16.6 million hectares of cultivated land, half of it taken up by sheep farms, a quarter by beef and dairy, 12 percent in plantations and just under 10 percent with mixed livestock. The remainder consists of horticulture, crops, deer farming and other enterprises. There are just under 70,000 farms, 65 percent of which are less than 100 hectares in size. Around three-quarters are worked by their owners and the bulk of the rest are run by sharemilkers, who usually own the herds but not the land.

The quantity of New Zealand farm production is matched by its quality. The climate —

lots of sun and regular rainfall — goes a long way to provide excellent conditions for livestock, while efficient management, grazing programmes, fertilisers and stock control make the most of the land. As a result New Zealand agricultural products are highly regarded throughout the world.

New Zealand farmers have also gained a reputation as world leaders in farming techniques, particularly in the use of mechanisation. Milking machines, mechanical shearing equipment and other general machinery have all been pioneered on New Zealand farms. New Zealanders were also leaders in aerial topdressing and other forms of agricultural aviation. Farming efficiency and innovation is matched by the support industries. Breeding and fertility programmes continue to improve the stock, while technology plays a large part in dairy factories and freezing works.

Despite its size New Zealand is the world's second largest producer of wool. Nearly every region has some sheep farms, with the majority in eastern areas of both islands. Sheep are also particularly suited to the hilly country of many areas. Merinos were the first breed to arrive in the 1830s, but Romneys make up the bulk of the modern sheep population.

New Zealand has around five million beef cattle and just under four million dairy animals. Three-quarters of the beef farms and 90 percent of dairy farms are in the North Island. Aberdeen-Angus and Hereford breeds make up most beef production, while the dairy industry relies on Friesian and Jersey breeds. Only about ten percent of dairy production is consumed locally with the rest being exported, primarily as cheese, butter, and milk powder.

In addition to traditional livestock farming, deer and goat farming have grown in importance. Just under one million deer are farmed for venison and around 1.3 million goats are bred for their fibres.

Horticulture accounts for around five percent of all exports, led by kiwifruit and apples. Most pip, stone and berry fruits can be grown in New Zealand and are also exported. There are over 200 wineries, and in 1995 around 60 million litres of wine was produced. New Zealand's sauvignon blanc, chardonnay, pinot noir and cabernet wines have all gained international respect.

Alongside horticultural plantations, New Zealand has a significant and growing forestry industry. Five percent of the country is covered by commercial forests. The felling of native trees is strictly regulated and the industry is based on introduced trees, 90 percent of which are radiata pine. Pulp and paper products dominate exports, while nearly all domestic needs for wood products are met locally.

Because New Zealand is totally surrounded by ocean it also has a large fisheries zone, around fifteen times the land area of the country. A quota system, available only to New Zealand individuals or companies, regulates catch size and tries to maintain stock levels. While quotas are only available to New Zealanders, about half of all commercial fishing is carried out by foreign ships either chartered by New Zealand companies or in joint ventures with them.

Industry and Energy

Manufacturing industries have become more important in recent years, with about 40 percent of exports being manufactured goods.

Due to the country's agricultural strength most industry is based around rural production. Food processing employs more people than any other industry. Much of this industry is concerned with domestic production, and exports of engineering products are at about the same level as processed food.

The bulk of local industry is a diversified mixture of small to medium-sized enterprises. Consumer appliance producers compete successfully in both domestic and export markets. Textiles and clothing industries take advantage of New Zealand's large wool and livestock production. High quality carpets, clothing and leathergoods are produced both for export and for local consumption.

New Zealand has also developed industries specialising in lifestyle products. Its recreational boating industry has gained world renown, New Zealand is a world leader in yacht design and production, and the jetboat was invented by a New Zealander. Other recreational industries specialise in adventure sports equipment and clothing.

The national reputation for innovation, especially in farming, has made New Zealand a leader in agricultural, horticultural and food processing technologies. In recent years it has also gained an increasing reputation for electronics and telecommunications technology, in particular for business and educational computer software.

New Zealand does not have many mineral resources and consequently there are only a few heavy industries. The aluminium smelter near Bluff, at the bottom of the South Island, accounts for around three percent of exports, but its raw materials are actually imported from Australia. There are two steel producers using ironsands and scrap, but stainless steel is generally imported and fabricated locally for use in agricultural, chemical and forestry industries.

Clean, renewable resources are the focus of New Zealand's energy needs. Hydro-electric schemes produce over 70 percent of all the country's electricity needs. Rivers running from the Southern Alps provide three-quarters of this hydro-electric power, while in the north the Lake Taupo catchment area and dams on the Waikato River make up the bulk of the rest. Extensive underground schemes are a feature of New Zealand's hydro-electric production in the South Island and central North Island.

Taking advantage of New Zealand's geological uniqueness, geothermal stations in the North Island provide seven percent of electricity production. The rest is provided in steam turbine stations powered by coal and natural gas. Experimental wind, wave and solar power schemes provide a limited amount of energy.

New Zealand is self-reliant for its electricity needs and 70 percent self-sufficient for all energy. However, most petrochemical products must be imported. Natural gas deposits off the coast of Taranaki produce synthetic petrol, methanol, and ammonia-urea, but this is only a supplement to the imported fuels.

Science and Technology

Technology is becoming a significant part of New Zealand life. New Zealanders are embracing the information technology explosion and today nearly a quarter of all homes have personal computers, compared with 1986 when less than seven percent had PCs. Cellular phone coverage is almost total.

Information technology has also improved to the extent that New Zealand is on the verge of the cashless society. Automatic direct crediting of salary, rent, and mortgage payments has

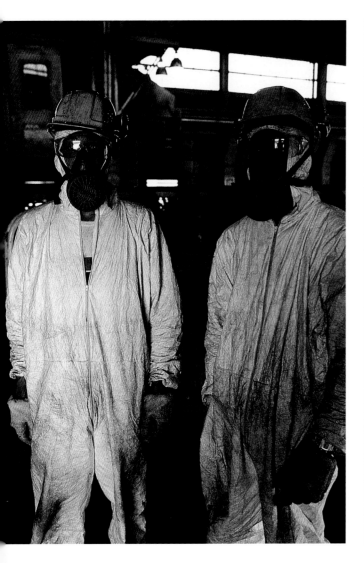

been commonplace since the late 1980s, and electronic banking by phone is now offered by all major trading banks. Electronic banking has expanded even further into retail businesses, and most stores now have facilities for EFTPOS (Electronic Financial Transaction at Point Of Sale). The plastic bankcards used in automatic teller machines can now be used in petrol stations and supermarkets. Most retail outlets, clothes stores, florists, and so on, offer EFTPOS, as do most corner shops.

Government-funded scientific research through the Ministry of Research, Science and Technology is an important aspect of the economy. There are nine Crown Research Institutes (CRIs), specialising in different aspects of New Zealand industry, such as horticulture, fisheries, meat and wool production. The CRIs compete for government and commercial funding with New Zealand's seven universities and a number of independent institutes.

The gateway to Auckland's Aotea
Centre, the work of Maori artist
Selwyn Muru.

Te Reinga to Auckland

Tradition has it that Northland is where Kupe, the Maori discoverer of Aotearoa, landed. When he took the news back to the legendary Hawaiki it was of a place of sunshine, beauty and incredible potential. The east coast is a complex of deep harbours with names that roll off the tongue like breakers coming in from the sea — Parengarenga, Houhora, Kerikeri — down to Whangarei, the main city of the north. The west coast is a maze of estuaries and shallow harbours, dominated by the Hokianga Harbour. Everywhere there are long sandy beaches and small sun-baked settlements snoozing in the sun.

Once upon a time the rugged hills were totally covered with the kauri, King of Trees; although the majority were felled for the early shipbuilding industry there are still some stands remaining to remind us of the imposing forests that touched the sky. Other places are haunted with memories of the kauri gumlands, where Maori and Dalmatian worked together.

The Bay of Islands was the cradle of both Maori and Pakeha settlement and it was here that the Treaty of Waitangi was signed in 1840. From the grounds of the Treaty House you can look across to Paihia and Russell. Nearby Okiato was the site of New Zealand's first capital, although this was soon moved to Auckland.

Sprawled across the isthmus between the Manukau and Waitemata Harbours, Auckland has grown from a shantytown on the beach to become New Zealand's largest city, and the largest Polynesian city in the world.

Today Auckland is in fact four cities — Auckland City itself, North Shore City, Manukau City and Waitakere City. The centrepiece of Auckland City is Queen Street, which runs up from the harbour to Karangahape Road, but throughout there are suburbs of distinctive charm and individuality. The dance clubs and restaurants of Ponsonby, Herne Bay, Parnell, Mission Bay and Devonport are always busy, while the Polynesian markets of South Auckland are vibrant and alive.

Auckland's natural configuration is complicated by volcanic cones, the most dramatic of which is Rangitoto Island. More than any other feature, Rangitoto is a physical icon for Aucklanders, symbolising their love of the outdoors and their wonderful harbour.

Native flax provides a graphic
foreground to the Hokianga Harbour,
on Northland's west coast.

Kerikeri was the second Anglican
mission station in Aotearoa New
Zealand, and the Stone Store is the
oldest surviving stone building in the
country. Nearby are the beautiful
Rainbow Falls. Orchards abound near
Kerikeri, the country's premier citrus-
growing area.

Once a haven for tall whaling ships, the Bay of Islands is still a favourite destination of sailors, sunseekers and fishers. Cruises include the Fullers Mailboat, which delivers mail to the more isolated bays of the coast, and the fascinating Hole in the Rock. Later on, where better to relax than Russell's historic Duke of Marlborough Hotel?

The sundial on Russell's Flagstaff Hill overlooks the town and the superb Bay of Islands.

Pompallier House, which stands on Russell's waterfront, is now a museum illustrating the early days of Russell and the French mission which was based here under Bishop Pompallier. Traditional printing crafts are now undertaken here, recreating the mission's major activity last century.

The seagoing waka, or canoe, Nga
Tokimatawhaorua, in the canoe house,
Waitangi, and the interior of the meeting
house on the grounds of the Treaty
House at Waitangi.

Auckland is New Zealand's largest city. The Sky City Tower is a dominant part of the skyline at 328 m, taller than both the Eiffel Tower and the Centrepoint Tower in Sydney. Sitting astride the Waitemata and Manukau Harbours, Auckland is a boaters' paradise

Built in 1929, Auckland's Civic Theatre is an architecturally elegant host to both movies and moviegoers. Further along Queen Street a pavement artist attracts a crowd who admire his work.

The city is connected to the North Shore
suburbs by the Harbour Bridge, built in
1959, with extra lanes added by Japanese
engineers (and wittily referred to as 'the
Nippon clip-on').

From the volcanic cone of Mt Eden the
island of Rangitoto provides a sculpted
backdrop to the city below. On the
waterfront, open air performers delight
visitors at any hour of the day or night,
while at Kelly Tarlton's Underwater
World spectators travel through
transparent tunnels within a giant
aquarium.

The life of the city. Chic Parnell owes its charm and character to Les Harvey, known to all as Mr Parnell. The Topp Twins are another Auckland institution; a singing duo, they really are twins. Just off Queen Street, Vulcan Lane provides an opportunity to rest one's legs, and perhaps enjoy a fragrant espresso or cappuccino in one of the area's fashionable coffee shops. In the Domain, the Wintergarden provides relaxation of a different kind.

The spectacular Marokopa Falls, near
Te Anga, in the Waikato.

Waikato to the Volcanic Plateau

During the Land Wars of the 1860s the Maori King Tawhiao threw his hat on a map of New Zealand and said, 'Where the hat lands I will protect all those who have given offence to the Queen of England.' The hat landed on the King Country, an area of limestone, which accounts for its often amazing topography of crags, ravines, canyons and caves. One such formation has become one of the great subterranean wonders of the world — the Waitomo Caves. The spectacular Glow-Worm Grotto shimmers with a million tiny lights like a miniature heaven.

The stronghold of the Maori Kings is in the Waikato on the Turangawacwae marae at Ngaruawahia. Not far away is Taupiri Mountain, where the Maori Kings are buried. Through this landscape winds the mighty Waikato River. Each year in March war canoes sail on the river as part of an annual celebration of Kingitanga, the heritage of the Maori King movement.

Right at the heart of the North Island is the Volcanic Plateau. The volcanic area actually runs from White Island on the east coast diagonally through Rotorua down to Taupo and the mountains of Tongariro National Park.

At Whakarewarewa Village, in Rotorua, Maori culture forms part of a theatrical backdrop of mudpools, hot springs, drifting steam and spouting geysers. If you want to be reminded of a more ferocious aspect of the area visit Waiotapu or the Waimangu Valley. In this region, in 1886, Mount Tarawera erupted, destroying the fabulous Pink and White Terraces. Drive on to Taupo, and when you swim in the lake, go yachting or fish for trout, just remember that once upon a time this was a volcano that blew its top.

A Maori sentinel stands to welcome visitors to the Ohaki Maori village on the approach to the Waitomo Caves.

At Waitomo, in the King Country, sightseers come from all over the world to visit the magnificent Waitomo Caves, one of the world's natural wonders. The traditional boat journey will take you through the caves, or you can join a blackwater rafting tour to explore this underground world in more adventurous fashion.

The city of Rotorua, with its ever-present smell of hydrogen sulphide, is at the heart of a region known for its spectacular volcanic beauty. Among its many attractions is the historic bathhouse in the Government Gardens, home of the Rotorua Art and History Museum. Also of interest is the Agrodome, which regularly features demonstrations of sheep shearing and

94

og working. But Rotorua is not only a
ecca for tourists; its setting enables
cals to enjoy lakeside living beside one
the many lakes in the area.

Rotorua's Whakarewarewa Reserve is a major centre of Maori culture and has become an important school of learning for Maori craftsmen and women. At its entrance visitors practise the hongi, the traditional Maori greeting. The carvings on the meeting house have a special significance for the local people.

The Te Arawa people are well known for their spectacular singing and dancing. Women practise the art of poi dancing and men perform the haka. Traditional stories are told in the movements and actions that accompany the songs.

The area around Rotorua boasts an amazing variety of thermal activity. While the geysers and mudpools at Whakarewarewa (opposite, bottom) are well known, a visit to the Wairakei Thermal Valley (opposite, top) just 10 km north of Taupo can provide an equally dramatic experience of steam and bubbling mud. Halfway between Rotorua and Taupo the colourful Champagne Pool (above) is one of the attractions of Waiotapu Scenic Reserve.

Across Lake Tarawera can be seen the famous Mt Tarawera, which on 10 June 1886 exploded, destroying the fabulous Pink and White Terraces.

Steam rises from the Wairakei
geothermal power station, the second
largest in the world. The awesome
power of the earth's natural resources
can also be seen at the mighty Huka
Falls, on the Waikato River, a little
nearer Taupo.

New Zealanders and visitors from all
over the world come to fish the waters
of Lake Taupo and ski the slopes of Mt
Ruapehu, whose warm crater lake looks
deceptively quiet in the afternoon sun.
Although the mountain has not erupted
in recent times, it is still an active
volcano. At the foot of the mountain
stands The Grand Chateau, with Mt
Ngauruhoe beyond.

Mt Ngauruhoe at sunrise, obscured by
the swirling clouds.

Late afternoon near Port Jackson,
Coromandel Peninsula.

Coromandel to the Wairarapa

Before the coming of the Pakeha, Coromandel provided an impenetrable screen of lush fern and kauri forest. Like the Northland forests, however, the kauri of Coromandel were soon felled for the ship-building industry. Gold was discovered at Thames and Waihi in 1867, and the gold industry flourished until early this century. Today gold is once again being mined at Waihi, but Coromandel is better known for the golden sand of its beaches and the wild beauty of its peninsula.

The shoreline of the Bay of Plenty can take your breath away, especially when pohutukawa blossoms in the summer. When Europeans settled the area it was developed into sheep and cattle country, but today oranges, kiwifruit and grapes have taken over. The harvest is shipped to markets around the world.

South of the Bay of Plenty is East Cape. For a time whaling flourished along the coast, but today's pursuits are primarily fishing, sheep and cattle grazing, and forestry. The settlements haven't changed much since the old days, resembling frontier towns out of a Western movie.

The beaches around the Cape, Poverty Bay and down through Hawke's Bay are among the most magnificent in New Zealand, and the whole coast resonates with history, both Maori and Pakeha. Some of the biggest Maori meeting houses are found here, and some of the North Island's most graceful colonial houses.

Inland from the Cape are the mysterious Ureweras, home of the Tuhoe people, the Children of the Mist. Their kingdom is a mountain fortress guarded by rocky terrain, silver waterfalls and lakes.

Hawke's Bay is the home of some of New Zealand's great sheep stations. More recently its climate has encouraged diversification into horticulture, market gardening and orcharding. Half of New Zealand's wine is made in Hawke's Bay. The twin cities of the area, Napier and Hastings, were severely damaged in an earthquake in 1931. Napier was reconstructed in the angular, jazzy, Art Deco style and today is known as the Art Deco Capital of the World.

Then there's the Wairarapa, the centre of New Zealand's Scandinavian community, and a strong agricultural region. The main city of the Wairarapa is Masterton, while nearby Martinborough is the centre of a growing wine industry.

The deserted peace of Cathedral Cove,
near Hahei, on the Coromandel
Peninsula, contrasts with the gentle
clamour of a livestock auction at nearby
Coroglen.

Driving Creek railway, the creation of
potter Barry Brickell, winds up through
the brilliant green of the bush to a view
across the Coromandel valley.

The east coast of the Coromandel
Peninsula looks straight across the ocean
to the place where the sun rises. Here at
Opoutere the sunrises are dramatic, with
colours ranging from delicate ochres and
pinks to cerise, violet and vermillion.

The fishing boat *Gay Dolphin* tosses in
Coromandel Harbour in a sea
quickening with the tide. At Thames
memories abound of the gold rushes of
the 1860s and '70s, when the town's
population reached 20,000, almost twice
that of Auckland. The Brian Boru Hotel,
one of the few remaining
accommodation houses, is best known
today for its Murder Mystery weekends.

White Island, in the Bay of Plenty,
occasionally sends up steam and lava
just to remind us that it is still an active
volcano.

Mt Maunganui, famous for its surf, is a favourite summer holiday spot in the sunny Bay of Plenty.

On the wall of a fish and chip shop at Katikati, a family poses outside a typical Bay of Plenty church, as if waiting for a photograph to be taken. On the beach near Opotiki, two Maori seek the succulent pipi, a shellfish regarded as a delicacy.

The East Coast has a relaxed lifestyle,
and the drive around the coast is for
those with plenty of time, who are
happy to leave themselves open to
whatever happens next. The locals
usually have time for a friendly chat.
During cultural practice at Apanui
School, Te Kaha, a young girl grins with
enjoyment and fun, and boys try to
come to grips with the finer points of
the haka.

A dolphin leaps during a sea world display at Marineland, Napier, one of several attractions on the city's waterfront. Cape Kidnappers, a short drive from Napier, is home to a colony of about 5,000 gannets. Some people walk around the coast to the colony; others prefer to be driven all the way.

Castlepoint Lighthouse, east of
Masterton, signals a warning to ships off
the wild Wairarapa coast. A fishing boat
shelters in the lee of the headland.

Two trampers in Whanganui National
Park, near the Bridge to Nowhere.

Taranaki to Wellington

On a clear day, Taranaki (also known as Mt Egmont) can be seen from the South Island. It made itself known to the earliest Maori canoe voyagers but when Abel Tasman sailed past in 1642 it hid itself from him. However, for James Cook in 1770 Taranaki was kinder. He saw it through cloud and rain, with lightning dancing around its crown. In 1841 ships of the New Zealand Company arrived from England's Plymouth and, within the gaze of Taranaki, established the settlement of New Plymouth.

From the summit of Taranaki you feel as if you can see the world. Ruapehu, Taranaki's brother mountain, is eastward. Seaward is a curve of black sand, like a fin flicking at the deep blue of the Tasman Sea. Below, the rainforest carpets the flanks of the mountain, and beyond the plains roll towards New Plymouth and Hawera to the south. Offshore, oil rigs dot the Taranaki Bight.

To the south, the deep gorges, waterfalls and wilderness of the Whanganui River have a special attraction for those who would explore it by canoe, white-river raft or jetboat. The Rangitikei and Manawatu rivers, further inland, are just as stunning. At the seaward end of the Manawatu gorge is the largest city of the plains, Palmerston North. For many years a university town, today Palmerston North is also a centre for agricultural and horticultural research, and for wider education.

Wellington, the capital, is one of New Zealand's most cultured and vibrant cities. The suburbs of Wellington all retain their own special character. Newtown, for example, is a mix of Maori, Pacific Island, Greek and new immigrant families, creating a joyful blend of fun and excitement. In recent years the waterfront and inner city have been transformed into a showcase of art, music, theatre and culture. Innovative architecture has added a new and exciting look to the city, contrasting with the older, gentler areas of Mount Victoria and Tinakori Road.

Mt Taranaki, also known as Mt Egmont, is New Zealand's most climbed mountain and the centrepiece of Egmont National Park. The mountain is a volcanic cone, sculpted into its present shape by past eruptions. Below the steep upper slopes dark forest takes over, in turn giving way to the softer colours of the Taranaki farmland.

Whanganui National Park, which opened in 1987, encompasses 79,000 hectares of lowland forest on both sides of the Whanganui River. The Park is popular with trampers, many of whom head for the Bridge to Nowhere. Built in 1936, the bridge was never fully utilised as many settlers were abandoning the area by the time of its completion. Today the area's main industry is tourism, and the river provides exciting jet-boating and canoeing adventures.

Low sun illuminates Oriental Bay, one
of Wellington's most attractive suburbs.

Wellington's Beehive is an addition
to the old Parliament Buildings.
Opened in 1981, it was inspired, so
people say, by the logo on a box of
matches.

The Cable Car provides a swift,
steep ride from the inner city, seen
here from Tinakori Hill, to the
university suburb of Kelburn.

The Wellington skyline has been transformed in recent years, with a number of striking new buildings. Wellingtonians are particularly proud of their Civic Square, with its paved courtyard and tiled fountains. The metallic nikau palm is one of several that surround the Wellington City Library. The library's curvilinear glass walls reflect light from a tiled pool.

The Marlborough Sounds offer glorious
isolation, a calm haven in which to
escape from the pressures of the world.

Marlborough and Nelson to Kaikoura

The Marlborough Sounds are magical sea-filled valleys which provide spectacular sailing and swimming. Their shores are clothed with unspoilt bush. Some of the islands further out are home to New Zealand's tuatara, a living link back to the dinosaurs of old.

Inland from the Sounds, the perspective changes. High tussock and alpine country overlook gentle river valleys and the sprawling Wairau Plains. Marlborough was once the home of great sheep stations, but today orchards, vineyards and berry fields dominate the landscape. The soil, and the sun, are particularly conducive to fine wine production and as a result Marlborough is home to some of New Zealand's best, and biggest, wineries.

West of Marlborough is Nelson, described by Abel Tasman in 1642 as 'a great land uplifted high'. Nelson shares with Blenheim one of the best climates in the country. Its beaches are golden sand swept by sparkling sea, the townships are colourful and friendly, and fruit trees, vines and berries flourish amid valleys of trees and ferns.

Nelson City, established by the New Zealand Company in 1842, is the centre of the province. Today it is a delightful mix of modernity and old world charm. Although its traditional industry remains horticulture, the area's rich fishing grounds have now turned Nelson into the biggest fishing port in New Zealand. The city is also a magnet for artisans — jewellers, potters, glassworkers and sculptors — who create some of New Zealand's finest craftworks. Close by is Abel Tasman National Park, a wonderful area of golden beaches, steep granite formations, limestone caves and native forest.

The Kaikoura coast follows the Pacific seaboard all the way down to Canterbury. Whaling was once a major industry along the coast. Today, the more gentle art of whalewatching provides an opportunity to witness some of the world's most beautiful creatures.

142

The hills surrounding the Marlborough Sounds are dotted with holiday homes, many of them reached by boat. During the still evenings the area is alive with the sounds of sea and forest. Among the most distinctive songsters of the region is the weka, a small flightless bird about the size of a domestic hen.

Lake Rotoroa, the larger of the two
lakes of Nelson Lakes National Park.

The sun, surf and wind make Abel
Tasman National Park ideal for
yachting, windsurfing and sea kayaking,
or simply lazing on its lovely beaches.

Many who visit Kaikoura come by train, enjoying the scenic coastal route. The area is famous for its kai moana, or seafood.

The view from Mount Fyffe, named
after a pioneer whaler. Today it is whale
watching that draws visitors to
Kaikoura, as well as adventure activities
such as paragliding.

Farmland falls to sea at Akaroa
Harbour, Banks Peninsula.

Christchurch and Canterbury

The landscape of Canterbury is dominated by its mountains. They are sentinels of the southern sky, with passes like narrow gateways through to the West Coast. For the traveller they provide an everchanging vista of immense power and beauty. New Zealand's longest glacier, the Tasman, is located in Mt Cook National Park. Ski-planes regularly set down skiers at the top of the glacier for a fabulous run down a magical river of ice and snow.

The immense Canterbury Plains, once the home of the giant moa, seem to roll on forever. From the air, the plains look like a vast pastoral ocean of patchwork green and gold, interrupted every now and then by the blue-grey of an intricately braided river.

In 1840 the French established a settlement at Akaroa, on Banks Peninsula, a township which today still maintains a piquant Gallic flavour. But it wasn't until 1848 and the establishment of the Canterbury Association in London that the idea of founding an Anglican settlement in New Zealand was formulated. Two years later, in 1850, four ships — the *Randolph*, *Charlotte Jane*, *Cressy* and *Sir George Seymour* — landed at Lyttelton. The idea was to transpose a model English society, complete with bishop, gentry, tradespeople and other workers, people known for their respectability and high morals. The result was a South Seas version of Britain that has no parallel in New Zealand.

Nowhere is this more apparent than in Christchurch, the largest city of the South Island. The cathedral triumphs in the centre, and church spires spike the sky. Amid drifting willows the river Avon wends its way through a city of Gothic architecture and ever-changing colours. The green banks and parks blossom with flowers in spring, transforming the city into a colourful garden. Walk around the old university buildings, now transformed into an Arts Centre, or visit some of the city's older schools, splendid amid leafy settings, and you would think you were in an English university town.

There is, of course, also a 'new' Christchurch, vibrant and ambitious, which reminds you quite firmly that the city is looking very much to the future. A busy airport, a growing reputation as an industrial city utilising the best of modern technology, and progressive city planning have made Christchurch one of the most positive of New Zealand's cities.

Cambridge? No, punting on the River Avon, Kiwi-style. The river winds its way through the city of Christchurch, past the modern Town Hall with its ingenious fountain, and the nearby Floral Clock.

Christchurch's Cathedral Square is always alive with activity. Buskers entertain, people sit and watch the crowds pass by, and the city's Wizard declaims.

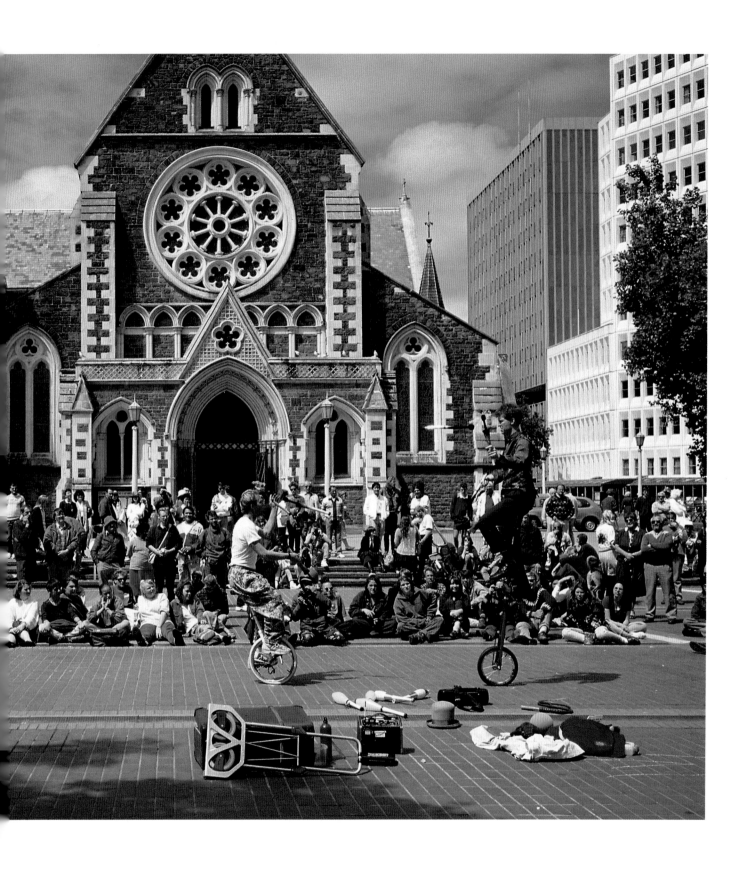

A prominent landmark in Lyttelton is the Timeball Station, its Victorian mechanism signalling the time to ships in the harbour by the dropping of a ball down the mast on the top of the tower.

Christ's College, founded
on the principles of an
English public school, is
one of the country's
oldest.

Two cyclists on Summit
Road, the rim of the Port
Hills, watch the sun set
over Christchurch.

159

A large mural, painted on the side of
the Fire Station at Lake Tekapo,
acknowledges the place of sheep in the
colourful history of the Mackenzie
country.

The Church of the Good Shepherd, at
Lake Tekapo, was built in
acknowledgement of the sacrifices of the
early runholders of the area. The
sheepdogs of the Mackenzie country are
also honoured here.

Sheep graze on winter pasture beside
Lake Tekapo, South Canterbury.

Scenic flights over the Alps are popular.
A plane appears as a tiny speck of
colour above the vastness of the mighty
Tasman Glacier, and a helicopter lands
at the head of the glacier.

Mt Cook National Park covers 70,000
hectares of the Southern Alps, and 65
kilometres of mountain chains.

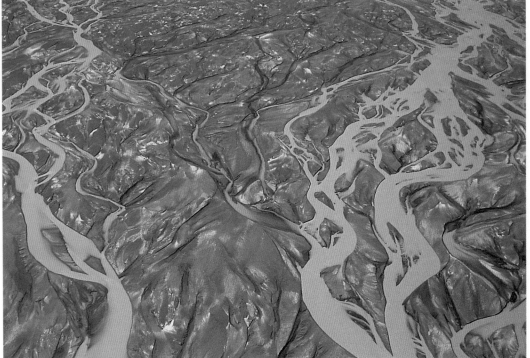

From the snow-capped peaks and
glaciers, water drains into the braided
rivers on both sides of the Main Divide,
and forms lakes such as Pukaki, a vital
part of the Upper Waitaki Power
Development Scheme.

A glimpse of what lies ahead, the
coastline of the West Coast.

The West Coast

The West Coast is rather like a forest fortress, its mountain peaks palisades guarding against all-comers. A constant curtain of rain provides an extra layer of protection. Were it not for the fabled greenstone, or pounamu, perhaps the Maori would never have come here, to the great Westland rivers, the Arahura and the Taramakau.

Later, another kind of stone, gold, brought Europeans into the area. Ironically, the gold was found beneath a greenstone boulder by Maori who were more interested in the pounamu. This was in 1864. A year later gold mining began in Hokitika and Reefton. Even later, another mineral, coal, added to the region's prosperity.

The goldmining days brought a sense of the frontier to the West Coast. Perhaps it is because of this that Coasters are considered different from other New Zealanders. Not any better or worse, just a bit different — irreverent, enterprising, sometimes stubborn, but always decent. In many respects they are the archetypal 'good keen men' and independent women of New Zealand's ideal society, having a healthy disrespect for authority and relying more on their own sense of what's right and what isn't.

One of the most dominant features of the West Coast is the opalescent sea, which seems to carry on a constant love affair with the coast. The whole of the West Coast is a place of whispers, of sounds and mysteries, offering moments of sheer beauty as when a white heron feathers the air at its nesting place at Okarito.

It is also a place of immense silence. The beaches are unpopulated and the emerald green forests are isolated. Nowhere is the silence more profound than at the two rivers of ice — the Fox and Franz Josef Glaciers. Sometimes, in the gleaming half-light of day, they defy reality and render the surrounding landscape unreal also.

The astonishing Pancake Rocks, at Punakaiki, lie within one of New Zealand's newest national parks, Paparoa. Nearby the rich red of the pohutukawa flower adds a vivid splash of colour to the bush. A little further south, a cyclist sets out on the road to adventure.

During the latter part of the nineteenth
century Okarito was alive with pubs,
dance halls, casinos, banks and stores,
as miners flocked to join the search for
gold on the Coast. Today it is a quieter
place, sought for its detachment from
the world, and the allure of its
whitebait.

A canoeist shares the peace of Okarito Lagoon with a rare white heron, or kotuku. The only breeding ground of the kotuku is on the banks of the nearby Waitangiroto Stream.

Guided walking tours take visitors right
on to the magnificent Fox and Franz
Josef Glaciers. At close quarters these
shining rivers of ice ripple with blue and
green colours and reveal jumbled blocks
of ice.

Gillespies Beach is part of a rocky coast
that was once part of the gold rushes,
and the allure of the precious metal still
calls back resolute goldpanners.

The West Coast combines superb
natural beauty with an immense
diversity of flora — some of the species
in Westland National Park date back
over 160 million years.

The perfect reflections of Westland's
Lake Matheson in early morning light.

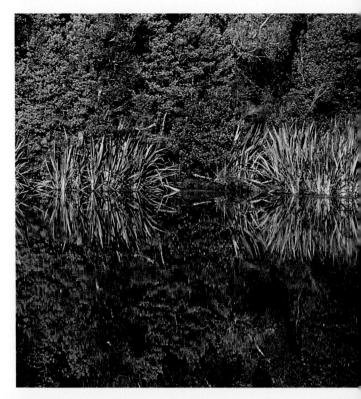

The West Coast is renowned for its extraordinary weather and skyscapes. Cloud swirls over Mt Tasman (below), and a rainbow emerges after a shower (right).

Winter landscape near Lindis Pass.

Dunedin and Otago

Otago is a place of mountains, lakes and glaciers. Most striking are The Remarkables, near Queenstown, but equally lovely are the mountains around Lakes Hawea, Wanaka and Wakatipu, where glaciers ground the hills into rounded shapes before the time of man. Then there is the Clutha, a river of immense strength, storming through steep gorges to the sea.

Queenstown is New Zealand's best-known mountain resort. An area of unsurpassable beauty, it is also a centre for adventure activities — jetboating, rafting, tramping, heliskiing or, for those who don't mind being tied by the ankles, the ultimate thrill — bungy jumping.

The earliest Europeans in Otago were whalers. As with Christchurch, however, settlers soon realised the potential of the alluvial plains, and in 1848 the ships *John Wickliffe* and *Philip Laing*, with three hundred settlers aboard, arrived in Otago Harbour. Primarily Presbyterian, the Scottish founders established Dunedin on the fortunes of great sheep stations. The discovery of gold boosted the city's coffers and, by 1871, one in every four settlers in New Zealand was to be found in Otago. By the 1880s Dunedin was the country's largest, most industrialised and pre-eminent commercial city. Although this is not the situation today, Dunedin still exerts considerable influence nationally.

Dunedin has the reputation of being the Edinburgh of the South, the result of its Scottish heritage. Constructed of grey stone, it is a handsome city, with many buildings that are perfect Victorian artefacts. Everywhere there are church spires topping churches of austere Gothic grandeur. The Municipal Chambers display a frontage in the Italian style, while the architecture of the law courts, the railway station and the university attest to a Victorian exuberance muted by a sense of respectability.

Throughout Otago there are still signs of a prosperity based on whaling, sheep rearing and gold. Otago's greatest treasure, though, is its unique landscape.

Lake Wanaka (above and centre left) and Lake Hawea (bottom left) are water-filled glaciated valleys, the result of glacier action that has smoothed and rounded the landscape below the surrounding peaks.

Rosehips and willows grace the
Matukituki river valley.

Mustering time at Loch Linnhe Station,
near Queenstown. Meanwhile, on the
banks of Lake Wakatipu, sheep briefly
take precedence on the road.

Queenstown is the home of adventure,
with bungy jumping and jet boating two
of its major attractions.

If a jump from the historic Kawarau
Bridge doesn't appeal, you can take a
gondola ride up to Bobs Peak, high
above Queenstown.

194

TSS *Earnslaw* is the last of four steamers that plied Lake Wakatipu during the height of the gold rush days. Queenstown nestles on the edge of the lake.

A sea lion, glistening sovereign of the seashore, roars at Moeraki Peninsula. The Moeraki coastline is steeped in Maori history, and the famed Moeraki boulders, each weighing several tonnes, are said to be the petrified food baskets of an early canoe which was wrecked on the offshore reef.

Taiaroa Head is the home of a famous
Royal Albatross colony. Also on the
Otago Peninsula is the imposing Otakou
Marae. A scenic rail journey in this part
of New Zealand must take in the craggy
Taieri Gorge.

The University of Otago was the first university in New Zealand. The old part of the building was begun in 1870.

Larnach's Castle, built in 1871 by a wealthy banker who later became a Member of Parliament, is notable for its impressive ballroom, ornate ceilings and Italian marble fireplaces.

Dunedin Railway Station, built in 1907, is embellished with an impressive tower, magnificent mosaic floor, and stained glass windows with a distinctly 'railways' theme.

Olveston is an Edwardian residence that conjures up the elegance of a bygone era, beautifully furnished with antiques, fine paintings and memorabilia.

Lush ferns in a remote Fiordland
setting.

Murihiku:
The South

The southern end of Aotearoa is known to the Maori as Murihiku, and encompasses Southland, Fiordland and Stewart Island. Southland's history is similar to that of Otago. Invercargill was settled by Scots people from Dunedin in 1856, and the Scots heritage is still noticeable in the way Southlanders speak; there is a distinct burr on their r's. The new settlers found Southland similar to the Scottish highlands, and they established sheep runs on the Southland plains.

Bluff is the harbour from which agricultural produce is sent to all parts of the globe. It is also a vigorous fishing port, with catches of deep-sea fish, crayfish and shellfish. The Bluff oyster is considered by connoisseurs to be the ultimate in oysters.

Offshore from Invercargill is Stewart Island, a special place of bush-clad hills and quiet beaches. The Maori name is Rakiura, a reference to the glowing skies and auroras which play on the southern horizon.

West of Invercargill the vista opens out to the unparalleled beauty of Fiordland National Park. Sea and the massive forces of the Ice Ages have created astounding physical configurations to the land. Every day rain, wind, cloud and sleet combine to recreate an everchanging panorama. Along the coast are the great fiords — Milford, Bligh, Caswell, Nancy, Doubtful, Dusky and Preservation Inlet. Inland are the Takitimu Mountains and the lakes Te Anau and Manapouri, and the magnificent Milford Track, a walk which has been called the finest in the world.

The superb Catlins coast has a rugged
grandeur that, once experienced, is
never forgotten.

Nugget Point lighthouse surveys a rocky coast. In contrast, the small church at Waikawa is serene in the sunshine.

Sheep shearing is a fast and furious business — definitely not for the faint-hearted.

A field of wild flowers on the road to
Milford Sound. Milford is dominated by
Mitre Peak, rising steeply from the deep
waters of the fiord.

Trampers experience all types of conditions on the 54-kilometre Milford Track, often described as 'the finest walk in the world'. The magnificent Bowen Falls drop down into Milford Sound.

Dawn at Cascade Cove, Dusky Sound,
and half-light at Acheron Passage.

Doubtful Sound, named Doubtfull
Harbour by Captain Cook in 1770, is
one of the most haunting of the
numerous southern fiords. Nearby,
morning mist hovers over the rainforest.

A playful dolphin leaps before the
Milford Wanderer, scouting across the
mist-shrouded waters of Dusky Sound.

216

No matter where you are, you will
always find surfers chasing the waves,
even here at Oreti Beach, among the
most southern waves of the world.

The tuatara, often called New Zealand's living dinosaur. Southland Museum in Invercargill has the country's most successful breeding programme.

In Bluff, at the very bottom of the South
Island, Fred and Myrtle Flutey have
turned their house into a showcase for
the paua shell.

Stewart Island is a special place. Remote and sparsely populated, it has great appeal to trampers and others seeking peace and tranquillity. It also supports a vigorous fishing industry.

Stewart Island's Maori name is Rakiura,
aptly translated as 'island of glowing
skies'.

Acknowledgements

Text: pages 7–70 by Tim Plant; pages 71– 223 by With Ihimaera.

All photographs by Holger Leue except:
Alexander Turnbull Library: page 22 lower.
Ian Baker: page 82–83.
Museum of New Zealand Te Papa Tongarewa: page 56.
New Zealand Government: page 26.
Stephen Robinson: pages 17 top left and right, 18, 19, 20, 21 lower, 22 upper, 23 lower, 25, 33 left, 35 upper, 36, 39, 40, 42 lower, 43 lower, 47 upper, 49 lower left, 58 centre, 59 upper, 63 upper right and lower left, 64, 65 centre and lower, 66 lower, 67 right, 68, 69.
R. Slight: 43 upper.
Don Stafford: pages 31, 32 top and right.